AF225835

L. J. Martin

Against
the
Grain

How I sold over
$100,000,000.00
(*Yes, that's one hundred million*)
in product in one year!

And How I Learned to SELL books!

by

L. J. Martin

L. J. Martin

Published by:

Buttonwillow Books
48 Rock Creek Road
Clinton, Montana 59825

ISBN: 978-1-7344413-0-7

Table of Contents

Introduction

Do you want to be more successful?

Do you want to be a better provider for yourself and your family?

Do you want to be self-sufficient, self-reliant, and proud of yourself?

Do you want to be able to help your friends and family?

Well, if so, you've got to help yourself first.

It's a given…starting from ground zero, you can't help others until you help yourself.

Luckily, if you're an American, no matter how screwed up the economy, you still live in the go-to country in the world, and you still have the greatest opportunity to fulfill those dreams than that of any other human on this planet, outside of the good old U.S.A.

Hi, I'm L. J. Martin, and yes, I sold over $100,000,000.00 in real estate product in 1985, and don't know how many millions before that particularly exceptional year; and since, have written and sold, and helped my wife sell, many millions of books. And I assure you product is product, no matter if it's shoes or Shetlands ponies or super high rise apartment buildings…it's all the same.

Why, because human nature is human nature, no matter how many zeros are involved.

I was a California real estate broker for 35 years, a general contractor for 15 years, and an appraiser for 10 years before I tired of those vocations (and to be truthful never wanted to work that hard again) and became a full time writer. Not that writing's not hard work; it's as hard as you want it to be, much like selling. My wife was also a real estate broker for 15 years, and she and I decided to follow another dream after that hugely successful year of 1985.

How did I do it? Well, that's what this little tome is all about but first….

CAUTION, if you're afraid of hard work you're reading the wrong tome. I may be a lot more stupid than many who've had success in their careers, for I don't know how to be successful without lots of hard work.

Good luck, you ask? Right, the harder I work, the luckier I get. Bad luck, sure, I've had my share, but part of moving forward is forgetting about blaming any failure on bad luck, rather you attribute failure to be a learning experience, and it's a damn site easier to learn from a failure as from a success. Do you remember hitting your thumb with the hammer, or missing it and hitting the nail on the head? And like hitting your thumb with the hammer, failure is usually due to your own lack of skill and training. It's no ones fault but your own.

You think "this guy must have been born with a silver spoon in his mouth." Wrong, we were, in fact, lucky to have three spoons: one for my mother, and one each for my brother and me. In all the decades of my life, I've never been given anything but advice, and never taken a dime from the government, other than those days when my mother was forced to live in county housing. And free advice, many times, is worth just what you paid for it…nothing.

I'm proud of the fact I've never taken anything from the government and wish more Americans carried that pride with them…for it's the lynchpin and the keystone of success, self-reliance, self-worth, and independence.

How did I get from county housing—as I recall our rent was eight bucks a month—to a house in the shadow of Montana's beautiful Sapphire Mountains and a winter house in beautiful Prescott, Arizona?

If you want to know, keep reading.

When life hands you lemons, make lemonade!

L. J. Martin

Against the Grain

I gave a lot of thought to the title of this advice on 'how-to' and engaged in a lot of introspection on my own progress through life and upon what I did to succeed and, in doing so, realized that I many times took the path considered to be the rough and rocky trail, the uphill path, the way against the grain.

In high school in a tough agricultural and oil town, I decided to both wrestle and play football—at 145 pounds at the time, and with a lot of tough farm boys weighing over 250 I had lots more success at wrestling than football. However, I learned lots from both experiences. I had a football coach in my senior year who gave us some advice that has stuck with me since that decades ago time. He had been a professional for the Chicago Bears, a lineman, and his advice was simple: don't take the easy way. If an opposing lineman was blocking you, and you took the easy way around him, that was exactly what he wanted you to do. Why? Because his runner was going the other way, and you'd miss your opportunity to dump him, which was your job.

The easy way seldom led to success. The easy was seldom leads to success.

Thanks, Coach Paul Brown, for that became my mantra.

Another piece of good advice came to me from a friend my own age, who was successful far above and beyond others in our class. It, too, was simple, effective, and to the point.

After going to college, yet leaving in my third year to take a job, which, at the time, represented all the money in the world, the job soon came to an end.

Not because of my failure, but because of my success.

The small water company I was asked to take over had seven employees, and had belonged to an oil company before it was literally forced upon a developer for whom I'd been working part time while trying to keep up an Architectural major.

My employer wanted this small 700 connection water company to serve a new subdivision he wanted to build, and they refused. To make a long story short, they wanted to get rid of this unprofitable albatross (unprofitable because it was run by a huge corporation which had no interest in it) and forced him to buy it for $10.00 and other good and valuable consideration.

I was going to school and working part time for him as a draftsman, but had done some other work including driving around central California finding the most advantageous spot to build a convalescent hospital, a business in which he wanted to participate.

Why he asked me to take over this small water company is beyond me. I was barely over twenty, but I guess he saw a fire inside and thought I could do the job.

The company, as I mentioned, had seven employees to maintain only seven hundred water connections. It had a manager, a girl in the office, several maintenance men, and a pair of meter readers. I was paid well plus given a new three-bedroom bath and three quarter house to live in (on the site of the water pumps and tanks) and a car to drive. Hog heaven, to his boy not long married, with a child and another on the way, who'd come out of county housing.

After a week I determined that there was nothing being accomplished by the seven employees that I couldn't do myself, with major maintenance being farmed out to contractors (which was already being done by current management) so I fired them all.

Fired them all.

And I did so without asking the approval of the man who'd hired me.

Against the grain? You bet.

It didn't exactly make me popular in the small town into which I'd just moved.

The right thing to do? It was yet to be determined, and I came close to being fired myself, as it was a shock to my employer.

However, I did the work myself, with no more help from outside contractors than the prior year.

My 'office girl' became the first of the telephone answering machines, with a reel to reel tape recorder at its heart, and my wife upon occasion filled in.

First I discovered that over half the water meters were inoperable and consequently customers were being charged the minimum rather than for water actually utilized. I set up a program replacing and repairing a number of meters each week, and income rose.

Do you think I was popular in the neighborhood? Hardly. Customers found themselves paying four or more times for water than had been their history.

Against the grain? You bet. Complaints to the Public Utilities Commission went up proportionately.

I was faced with lots and lots of conflict— including a fistfight or two—over the one year I was a water company manager and it was a great learning experience.

Why only one year?

My employer was able to sell the water company to a large corporation which was in the water business for two hundred thousand bucks. Not a bad profit. I got a nice bonus and was offered another job with him, several hundred miles to the north, but during that year I'd been studying for my real estate license and had passed the test.

Going against the grain had paid off handsomely.

I had a few bucks in my pocket, and had advanced my opportunity by obtaining a license.

I wanted to go home to my ag and oil town where I knew the territory, at least the lay of the land and the neighborhoods.

"You can't lead anyone else further than you've gone yourself."
                                        Gene Mauch

L. J. Martin

Opportunity

Taking the job offered by my former employer would have been the easy way, but I chose to go against the grain.

Over confident? You bet.

As I mentioned, my older brother and I were raised by my mother, God bless her beautiful soul. My dad, for many, many years, loved John Barleycorn more than his family, so my mom detached us from him and went to work to provide for us.

I never saw a bitter tear from her, and I learned from that experience. If she had a fault, it was overconfidence in her boys. We were never told there was something we couldn't do, or there was something beyond our reach.

When I informed my mother that I was going into the real estate biz she, of course, encouraged me with "you're a natural born salesman."

I soon learned that there are no "natural born salesmen."

Selling is an acquired skill, just as being a fine carpenter or skilled mechanic.

But I was given opportunity. The friend I mentioned before, successful far beyond others in my class, now a partner in a real estate brokerage, gave me a job with the best company in my town, and I was the first hired there without two years of prior experience. Thank you, Lawton. I'm forever indebted.

Over confident? You bet.

Now all I had to do was become successful in something I'd never done, requiring skills I had not acquired, in a business in which you were totally on your own, with the exception of a few good souls willing to mentor when they had time, which was not often.

The first determination of whether or not you'll be successful is what you do with this intangible called opportunity.

Will you take advantage of each and every morsel handed you? Will you be in a position to take advantage? Or will you take the easy way, while the runner passes on the other side of that opposing lineman?

The fact is, no matter the old cliché, opportunity does not only knock once. For most of us, it knocks hundreds and hundreds of times during our life. The question is, will you risk confronting it?

Well, I'd confronted it by taking this sales job (I say job, but it was straight commission) and now the question was could I conquer it?

I worked six months without making a sale.

Failure? You bet.

But the opportunity was still there, and the question was do you learn from your failure?

I learned one thing, probably not soon enough as I was hard headed, thinking I was a natural born salesman, believing my sweet overconfident mother.

I was not a natural born salesman, I finally discovered after a long, frustrating, six months…, as there is no such thing.

You have to do what others won't, in order to achieve what others don't.

L. J. Martin

Taking Advantage

I'm often amused by those who demean salespeople.

Oh, he's just a salesman!

Do you know what the highest paid profession in the world is? Sales, of course.

Do you know what drives the economy of every free-enterprise, capitalist country in the world. Sales, of course.

Nothing happens in a free-enterprise country until somebody sells something.

Factories don't churn out goods, employees aren't hired, goods aren't consumed, until somebody sells something.

Sales are the pumping heart, the lifeblood, of our economy.

How much money do you want to make? Sellling allows you to make all the money you want; you just have to put yourself in the way of opportunity, and work, work, work.

So, here I am, six months into a new job, and failing miserably. So what to do about it?

First is analyzing the problem.

Second, fixing it.

An epiphany! The problem was, obviously, I didn't know ka ka about how to sell.

I was given the opportunity many times. Remember me saying that this friend hired me, a young guy like myself, he gave me some good advice?

That advice was simple, as is most good advice, and that was to be in the way of opportunity. I was in the most successful real estate company in my community, and it was full of some twenty salespeople, all of who had at least two years of successful experience before being hired. All were making money (except me), and all had some degree of comfort. They were all hard-working, but somewhat complacent. The advice I was given? Be the first one in the office.

Why?

That was before the time of cell phones, automatic call referrals, and the other technical advances enjoyed today by business and each of us.

The company did not even have an answering machine yet, and didn't open their doors until eight o'clock in the morning.

Like most in the real estate business, I started without a specialty and would sell anything, homes, lots, land, commercial, that came my way…but single family residence was by far the predominant opportunity.

And folks looking for a home are often in town living in a motel, waiting to get settled in both that new home and their new job. And they are up and at 'em early, and making phone calls on those newspaper adds, or for-sale signs they've seen, long before eight o'clock.

At my friend's advice, I hit the office before seven in the morning, and the phone rang with no one else to answer it.

Against the grain, in before the office actually opened.

Opportunity, you bet.

I put myself in opportunity's path, and it came, but it wasn't happening for me.

Taking advantage of it was another matter altogether.

So, what's this selling thing all about?

"You may have a fresh start any moment you choose, for this thing that we call "failure" is not the falling down, but the staying down." Mary Pickford

Selling

I sat with both partners in the real estate company, both successful guys, and spilled my guts, not as if it was something they didn't already know. I wasn't making any money, and had to do something.

What?

They knew I was in the office early and often the last one there. So, it obviously wasn't for lack of opportunity, in fact I may have well been hurting the company as sales were lost to other companies because I didn't close them.

Closing? What's that all about?

It's the key to turning opportunity into money.

And money, my friends, is how you keep score.

Money is how you help yourself, and remember, you can't help others until you help yourself.

So, let's figure out how to turn opportunity into money.

Both partners told me the obvious. I had to learn how to close.

The older of the two partners handed me a long play record album. "Closing the Sale." He told me if I learned the techniques therein, and applied them to all the opportunities I was given in his firm, I wouldn't have to worry about making money.

Okay, how to learn all those closing techniques.

Of course, I played the album…then played it again. I don't know how much time it took to listen to the full "long-playing" 33rmp album, but as I recollect, an hour or so.

I listened, but I wanted it ingrained in my brain. So I got one of those yellow legal pads, and began writing. I wrote, longhand, every word of that album.

Did I learn how to close?

The next opportunity I had, after showing a young couple only three houses, I closed the sale.

Amazed? You bet, no one was more amazed than I was.

One of the interesting things stated by the very successful salesman who'd taken the time to pass along his closing techniques was that the average salesman, making over one hundred thousand dollars a year (about seven times the national average at the time), closed his sale on the seventh closing attempt.

I hadn't been using one closing opportunity; no wonder I'd made a big fat zero in my first six months.

Was I a slow learner? You bet, and I felt plenty stupid. Mom, I loved you, still love you, but, man-o-man, were you wrong about his one.

There are no natural born salespeople.

Period.

29

"Remember, you only have to succeed the last time."
Brian Tracy

L. J. Martin

I Don't Need to Sell!

Oh, yeah, you don't need to sell?

Balderdash. We all need to sell, and had we some selling skills life would be much, much easier and far more rewarding a profitable.

Have you ever asked for a raise?

Do you think it important to use good sales techniques when you did so? If you don't think so, you're so very, very naive.

Selling is something each and every one of us have done hundreds of times in our life, be we declared salespeople or not. It's part and parcel of life, everyday life, for every one of us.

If you learn only one or two of the simple closing techniques I'm going to teach you, the techniques that helped me sell over one hundred million dollars in product in one year, you might have gotten that raise, or at least gotten it sooner and easier.

So if you think you don't need to sell, don't need to be one of those salespeople you've demeaned so many times, then you're not aware of what each and everyone of us does almost every day of our lives.

I want to go see the action adventure movie on at the local theater, and my wife wants to see the romance. Do I say, "No, dummy, those movies always make you cry." No, I do not, not if I really want to see the action adventure. I say, "Are you looking for a good cry, sweetheart?" or "Sure, I like to be sad and grumpy for a week or so. Remember that guy always kills off one or the other at the end of his books. How about a happy ending instead where the bad guys get their come'uppins?"

That's selling, admittedly inane and simple, but selling…and we all do it.

You do it, I do it, we all do it.

From there to negotiating with the boss over that raise, with the car salesman over the price, with our mother-in-law over where we're going to spend Christmas, at her house or my parents (if my parents were alive). With our child or grandchild over cleaning his room. We all sell, everyday, in some way.

You ask how can you be selling when your negotiating over *buying* a car? You're buying, not selling.

Again, balderdash. You're selling, but selling your side of the deal. You're selling the fact the car is maybe not exactly what you want so he should lower the price (even if you're dying to own it), you're selling the fact you have to have a lower interest rate or you're going to walk, and on and on. Each and every step of a negotiation is selling.

And as you'll learn, selling is not always talking. Sometimes the most powerful selling is not talking.

But more about that later.

"Self pity is an acid which eats holes in happiness."
Earl Nightingale

L. J. Martin

Closing?

Okay, so what's this closing all about?

And maybe even more importantly, why do we need to know how to 'close?'

And what is a close?

A close is getting an affirmative decision, a yes, and beyond that a contract or the passing of money. It's the affirmative consummation of a transaction. In real estate, it's the execution of a contract. Then normally you keep selling until the deed is actually recorded and title passes. In life, many times, it's merely getting your way.

We need to know how to close in order to get those items in the above paragraph to happen.

How many folks do you know who won't make a decision, who avoid, at all costs, making a decision?

Even when that decision is to their advantage?

All your life, if you're the typical human, you've been told, "Don't sign anything."

I'll tell you how to simply circumvent that objection in a while.

All your life you've been told, beware of salespeople, even though many, many times salespeople bring to you exactly what you need. Life insurance to protect your family in case of your untimely demise, a home that meets your wants and needs, an automobile that will be safer for your children and loved ones, or more efficient and less expensive to operate.

These folks need help making the right decision, and that's where a good closer enters the equation.

So, what's a close, to be more precise?

The most simple and straightforward close is the 'order book close.'

You're selling in a clothing store. A customer of average size walks in and asks, "Do you have any black socks?"

You don't say yes, you don't ask what size, you don't ask how much he wants to spend, you ask, if anything, how many pairs he'd like. Had he said, "Do you have a pair of black socks?" you wouldn't even ask that, as you know he wants only one pair.

You walk to the sock counter and pick up the average size pair of black socks then to the register or order book and begin writing.

That's an assumptive order book close.

After studying my how to close long playing record, I was called by a young couple I had known in high school, who asked me to show them some three bedroom homes. We're I shopping for a home,

I'd want to know everything in my price range in the area in which I'd want to live.

Don't have pre-conceived notions about what your customer/buyer/spouse/girlfriend/boss wants. He or she is he or she and you are you.

I showed this young couple three houses, went to their home, carried in my deposit receipt book, sat on their sofa, pulled out my pen, opened my deposit receipt book and asked, "Which one did you like the best," and to my great surprise, they answered, "The second one."

So I began filling out the deposit receipt, and when I came to the offering amount, asked, "What do you think you'd like to offer?"

And to my continued surprise, they replied with a number only slightly below the asking price.

In a month's time, I closed my first sale.

Closing works. They loved the house, my bosses and I loved the commission checks. Everyone was happy, including the seller.

In the next six months of that first year, I'd made more than the average income in the country for a whole year.

And all because I'd learned something about my trade.

Most real estate sales people would have shown them three houses then asked when they'd like to go out and see more.

I'd gone against the grain.

"Setting an example is not the main means of influencing others; it is the only means."

Albert Einstein

The Seventh Closing Question

Remember my saying that the long playing album said the average salesman who earned over one hundred thousand dollars a year, when the average income was ten thousand a year, made his average sale on the seventh closing question?

In order to do that you need to know a few more closing questions than the simple order book close.

Not that you can't do the same one over and over so long as it doesn't insult the intelligence of the part on the other side of the desk.

Most closes are easy, however some are more difficult:

The Ben Franklin Balance Sheet close is one which takes a little more time and finesse.

You are sitting across the table from Mr. and Mrs. Jones, and they are interested in the home/car/insurance policy/yacht/airplane or whatever it is you're trying to peddle. Or it's your boss, and you're trying to convince him to give you that much deserved raise.

So you pull out a piece of paper and say, "Let's list the pros and cons of this deal/car/policy, etc."

You make two columns, one the pro column, one the con.

And you help them with the pros, and keep your mouth shut with the cons.

You'll soon discover that your pro list is much longer than the con list.

You're closing question: "Golly, Mr. and Mrs. Jones, it looks like there's lots more reasons for you to own this than not."

The puppy dog close is a great one, but only works with certain products.

The example often used is a puppy, of course. A couple is in your pet store with their six year old daughter, who falls in love with the most homely puppy in the place. You know the Jack Smiths as they are regular customers, and know you can trust them. The daughter begs, "Daddy, daddy, let's buy this one, please, please."

Daddy says, "He's too young, honey. He'll widdle on the floor and you'll have to clean it up."

It's time for you to help with the puppy dog close. "Jack, I'll tell you what…take the little fella home and keep him for a couple of days. If you don't like him, return him and I'll give you your money back. Here, I'll even give you a five pound bag of puppy food…." And if you really want to put the pressure on Jack, you turn to his daughter and offer, "Sweetheart, you can take the puppy home for a while if you'd like."

Do you actually think that even when Rover has widdled on the kitchen floor four times, and Jack's had to clean it up, that he's going to disappoint his daughter, who's invited half the neighborhood children over to see her new puppy.

It's not going to happen, and Jack will soon be in with his credit card and to buy an additional fifty pound bag of puppy chow.

Why do you think new car dealers let you take a thirty or forty thousand dollar vehicle out for a test drive? They only pray that you brag to your neighbors or that the girl you want to date sees you driving that shiny new rod, or that your wife falls in love with the fact she can plug her iPod into the sound system.

That's the puppy dog close, and it works with a fifty dollar puppy or a two million dollar yacht.

And then there are at least a hundred closing opportunities for a product with multiple sizes, multiple colors, multiple prices for one reason or another. The opportunity here is to bring the customer to a buying decision, the ultimate decision, by him/her making a lot of simple but affirmative decisions.

He asks, "What color can I get it in?"

You don't answer by listing the colors, or handing him a color chart.

You ask, "What color would you like?"

When he says, "Red," you've got an affirmative answer, and if you happen to have a red one it's time to break it out and open your order book and start to write.

If he asks, "Doe's it come with the four hundred horsepower engine?"

You don't say, "Sure." You ask, "Would you like the four hundred horsepower engine?"

And on and on as you lead him, with his own affirmative decisions, to a close.

And how about that objection to the dreaded "Don't sign anything." I promised you I'd get to it. Most of us have heard it all our lives from our mother or father or from that helpful uncle, "Don't sign anything."

So, don't ask them to sign anything.

When you spin that order book or contract or deposit receipt around with the pen atop for easy use, you never, never, never, never, never say, "sign this."

Rather it's, "As you requested. Please approve this."

They are in charge, you're asking for their approval. They are not 'buying,' they are rather 'granting you' their approval.

And the odds are nine million to one that no one has ever told them not to approve anything.

Getting affirmative answers is a critical part of the process of closing. Simple questions like, "Are you with me so far?" or "Will this work for your family?" or "Is this a solution to your problem?" All either bring affirmative answers or an objection that you can generally overcome.

In regards to objections, if you want to close during this meeting, then it's important to solve your buyer's qualms. "Have I answered all your questions?" It's a question that moves you forward.

You can't always get all the questions, and of course you can't always make that sale on the first meeting. You might not have all the answers, or he or she might want to "think it over."

Call backs are a critical part of selling. And happen far too often. Your customer/client leaves with a "call me tomorrow."

Never, never, never call back and ask "Have you made up your mind?" It's an invitation for him or her to take the easy way, and the easy way is almost always a NO.

Never call back without new information. Never ask for a NO, ask for another affirmation. Never, unless there's no other way, try to close over the telephone. It's much harder for a person to shine you on if it's over the telephone, than when he's looking you in the eye and knows how hard you've worked to get him the right price on that automobile or show him the right house.

Go against the grain, drive to get face to face with your buyer, and ask another seven closing questions.

"Whatever good things we build end up building us."
Jim Rohn

The Wagging Tongue

One common misnomer about salesmen is that they have a gift of gab. It ain't necessarily so.

Some of the best salesmen I've known are stoic, and oft times the customer has to pry information from this tree-trunk of a guy. But when he talks, when the tree-trunk finally speaks, it's with a closing question.

And many times his seeming fault is in fact his greatest virtue as a salesperson.

The fact is, silence is the most powerful tool in the salesperson's arsenal.

Silence, is, in fact, the salesperson's number one pressure tool. When you think of high-pressure salespeople, you generally think of someone talking, talking, talking, when it fact silence is by far the highest form of pressure.

But you've got to know when to be silent, when to apply that pressure.

It's right after you've asked that closing question. For instance, the simple, "Cash or credit card?"

Then, it's imperative that you SHUT UP.

More potentially successful sales are lost because the salesperson talks rather than listens, than any other way. When you've asked a closing question, and you can't wait for the answer because you are more nervous than the buyer, you've let him or her off the hook. You asked, they don't have to answer, because you couldn't shut up long enough to let them.

Your wagging tongue just cost you a sale.

Many times your closing question will be answered with an objection. How can you hear that objection if your impatience has not let it be expressed? More importantly, how can you overcome an objection you've never heard?

You generally don't make sales without overcoming objections. Buyers don't buy unless objections are overcome.

The largest sale I ever completed was closed after I waited twenty three minutes, by my watch, from the time I asked the final closing question to the time my question was answered…in the affirmative.

I waited; he bought. I kept my mouth shut.

If you don't think twenty three minutes is an eternity, try waiting to see if you've closed a fifty million dollar sale while your customer is taking two phone calls, talking to his secretary, and staring out the window of the penthouse office in his fifteen story office building.

All while you're refusing to talk until he either answers your closing question, or posts another objection.

Silence is your friend, and your most powerful tool…but most of you reading this will not be able to stand the pressure.

"Whether you think you can or think you can't – you're right."   *Henry Ford*

L. J. Martin

Simple Selling

As a salesperson, my most significant accomplishment was certainly selling over one hundred million dollars in real estate product in one year…and a very difficult, down year at that. However, all selling is the same. In this segment I'm going to take in down to the lowest common demoninator, the industry in which I now work…books.

There's quite a difference selling a multi-million dollar piece of real estate, or a ten million dollar real estate loan, than selling a five buck book…or is there?

When I got into the book biz, I quickly learned that a great way to get your name out there was doing booksignings. So I became an expert at that sales effort, setting records way above those of far better known writers. Here's an article I did to show others how:

L. J. Martin

May I Sign That For You?
Or Booksigning 1A
How to do a successful booksigning!
by L. J. Martin

Booksignings.

To some authors, they're about as much fun as a root canal.

Booksignings, after the initial ego gratification of a first book, are a unique form of torture where one sits astride a cold metal chair in a corner of a musty book store while passerby's presume you're registering voters or offering petitions to "save the whales."

But they can be a career builder, sometimes even ego gratifying, and a way to *sell* books. To some of you, that concept, *selling* books, may be repugnant. In fact, selling anything may be repulsive to you. Having been a salesman all my life, it's second nature to me, and, by the way, it's also the highest paying profession in the world. To put it in your perspective, even Louie, D. Steel and S. King are pikers in the income department compared to some of this country's great salespeople.

Nothing happens in this free enterprise system of ours until *someone sells something*. Publishers can't pay the help, or buy manuscripts, or sponsor book tours unless someone is out there *selling* books.

And it's my belief that it's your responsibility as a major contributor to the book process to contribute to that effort--at least to not hinder it.

But selling, like writing, is a craft. A learned art that takes some practice.

The fact is your writing career can't grow unless your readership grows. So the more of your books you get into the hands of readers, the more opportunity you have to find a few who like what you do, and may just look for your next book without you personally shoving it into a reluctant hand.

There's only one primary reason to do a booksigning, and that's to *sell* books. Delbert, the bookstore manager at D. Balton has not gone to the trouble of stocking a case of your *Cruising the Strip Joints of Southern Louisiana*, of contacting your publisher or his own corporate office and getting that great poster made, of rounding up a table and chair and vase of plastic flowers because he wants your sparkling company for a couple of hours.

And Delbert sure doesn't want to re-pack and return forty five of the fifty books he's stocked because his "author" has elected to *read* a good book rather than *sell* his own while he or she's warming the booksigning throne. And you sure as hell don't want him to strip the covers off those paperbacks and irritate your sacred sell-through. For those of you not familiar with the term "sell-through," it's the percentage of books not returned (presumed sold) of those shipped. In the case of Westerns, many times that percentage is as low as 40%. And I'm sure you're aware that returning a book, when it's a paperback, means only returning the cover. The rest of the 250 pages go to the shredder.

But back to booksigning. Reading a good book is definitely the wrong way to do a booksigning.

Besides selling books, there is a secondary reason for doing a booksigning, and that's to *please a bookseller.* But trust me, you'll please and impress them more if you sell the hell out of those books.

If you don't want to *sell,* stay home. A signing is not an invitation to be idolized by an adoring public, it's a book*store* to which you've been invited. A bookstore, with rent and light bills and personnel costs.

Unless you're D. Steel or S. King, the likelihood of having a line of patrons salivating for a signature is slim-and-none and Slim's out of town.

So what do you do? You take advantage of every *live body* within polite (and sometimes not so polite) speaking range. And you can do that far better if you set four simple ground rules with the bookstore before you agree to sign.

1. Find the *right day* to sign. An event at the location of the bookstore, a sidewalk sale for

instance, that's the best day to sign. More people, more targets.

2. You have to have people to sell to in order to sell, so locating in the highest *traffic* area of the bookstore is best, and out on the sidewalk or in the mall walkway itself is even better. You want to send the guy who came to the mall for a pair of BVD's away with a book *and* a pair of BVD's. It's usually much easier to sell him a Western, than to sell one to the guy who came into a bookstore to buy a manual in order to pass his concrete contractor's exam.

3. You need the books *on the table*, not on the shelf, even if you're outside in the mall walkway. (You'll see why later)

4. You don't need a helper. Save the chat with the bookstore personnel until after the scheduled signing time. (He'll "step on your close," which I'll explain in a moment.)

Now it's up to you.

You've got the table, the prime location near the front entrance or out in the mall; a pile of books on hand; a great poster on the window behind you; and the manager and his employees, at your request, are leaving you to do your job. There are a lot of folks passing by, most intent on buying new underwear.

Now what?

Sell books, that's what.

All direct selling is an interchange between buyer and seller. Great salespeople sell to those who may *not yet know* they want to buy. You can't ask a closing question unless you establish a relationship, even the most tentative of ones, and you can't do that without talking--communicating.

Step one is letting them know *why* you're sitting on that cold chair.

Greet everyone who passes. "Hi! Are you a reader?" Or, "Do you read westerns?" Or, "Do you like strip joints?" Or whatever is applicable.

It's seldom you get a "no" to the first question. You do occasionally get "What do you think I am, an imbecile?" To the second you may get a straight out "no," then the question is, "How about your dad, or husband?" Or "An autographed book makes a great gift."

This is the easy part. "Good morning, are you a reader?" is an easy question, but not a closing one, and closing questions are *how* you sell. If you get the least encouragement, the next piece of selling business is to get the book in the buyer's hand. And you do that by handing it to him. "Have you read mine?"

This also informs him that you're not about to ask him to sign a petition. Even though you're sitting there with a pile of books and a poster, his mission was to buy a pair of skivvies or socks, so you've got to slow him down and make him *think* books. Let him read the cover copy. Don't talk while he's digesting the product. It, too, is there to sell.

Now *maybe* he gets it. You're an author.

"Did you write this?" is something near what his next question will be.

"Yes, it's a great guide if you're into strip joints," gives you a chance to relate to your buyer and his/her interests. The easiest sell is one that satisfies a need.

"Looks great," he says. . . .And now is when 99.99% of you *farm it out.*

Now what.

Step two. A close, that's what.

"May I sign that for you?" you ask, with your best smile.

It's decision time. The book is in his hand, he's already said it looks great. You've offered to autograph it. And more importantly, you've given him an easy question to answer. You haven't asked, "Do you want to part with a hard-earned $5.95 rather than have lunch?" That's a much tougher question to answer. His choice is replying, "No, doofus, I don't want your autograph," which is a little like saying "Who the hell are you?" Or admitting that he doesn't have the $5.95 until pay day. All tough ego-preventing responses to your *close.* A much easier answer is "yes."

You've asked your closing question, and he's silent for an interminable five seconds. . .and you know what 99.999% of you will do? You'll get sucked right into that maelstrom of torturous silence with, "That's a great belt." And you know what-- *you've let him off the hook.* Now he can tell you about his Uncle Charley who does leather work, and ignore your *close* while casually slipping the book back on the table. You've given him the easy out--right through your big mouth.

Don't ever forget that you're doing them a *favor* by selling them your book. If you don't believe that, stay home. Let someone else who believes in you, even if you don't, sell your books.

The largest real estate deal I ever sold, I waited in silence 23 minutes (by the watch) after asking a closing question. Now, when you're waiting for an answer that may mean a 50 foot sailboat or six bedroom house, 23 minutes seems enough time to read *War and Peace*. But, I knew the rule--first guy to speak loses. So I waited, and he took a couple of phone calls, looked out the window across San Francisco Bay for a while, and finally spoke--and I won, or should say "earned," the largest commission of my life.

You speak, and he's off the hook. Silence, is the salesperson's best friend. Silence is the loudest closing technique of all. Not chatter. But silence *after* a closing question. Silence is what separates the salespeople with yachts from those with yearning. That's why you don't need the help of the manager or store personnel. They can stand the pressure even less, and they'll speak into the silence. Hell, if they were *trained* to sell, they'd probably be making a lot of money somewhere else, not schlepping your books in a chain store while working their way through college so they can get as far from that bookstore as possible. They, in their well-meaning enthusiasm, will "step" on your close every time—by speaking and letting your buyer off the hook.

You can't get that book into their hands unless the books are on the table in front of you. If the bookstore owner is worried about someone hooking a book, then he doesn't think much of the value of your time. You might be better off staying home and working on your next, *Strip Joints of Northern Louisiana*.

Kat, my wife, and I make a game out of booksignings. A contest, with inner self to sell more than we sold the last time, and with each other. Sometimes the closing questions go a little overboard, such as the time I suggested to a haggard looking man that he was probably going to have a heart attack if he didn't relax with a good book. I lost that sale. But it was good advice. Or when Kat turned to a passing lady and asked, "Do you read?" before she noticed the red and white cane. To the lady's credit, she laughed even though she could not see Kat's red face.

But then again, we sold 650 books in six hours— three two-hour booksignings in three consecutive days. And made a lot of friends at Anderson News.

And not one of those folks who walked away from that table with a book in their hands knew Kat or Larry Jay Martin from Adam's off ox before that day.

Now they do.

A few other tricks to help you sell books for that hard-working bookseller.

Have a representation of all your titles on the table if you have more than one, not just your newest book—including a couple of your audios and large print titles, if you've got them.

Help him and yourself by providing him with press releases a couple of weeks in advance, or by offering to contact the press yourself and get those articles in the local paper. Sometimes large malls have their own newspapers! Sometimes military bases have their own papers, radio stations, and T.V. stations.

Sign all the unsold books before you leave. The bookseller is less likely to strip covers and return them if the books are signed. Chains will sometimes circulate those signed copies to other stores. And take and use your own "signed by the author" stickers.

Make sure some of your books remain on the shelves during the booksigning. Many times a shy customer will bypass you, but look for the book on the shelf or in the racks.

Don't presume your buyer realizes you're the author, even though you've got the book in his hand and *told* him it's yours. He thinks it's yours, as in ownership, and you want to *sell* it to him, not that it's yours, as in authorship, even through you still want to sell it to him. Many times he thinks you're a bookstore employee. Even these "not-so-quick-ones" may have the $5.95, and may become fans. Usually they're not really slow, just distracted by the need of a new pair of BVD's.

If you're selling a Western, don't be bashful about calling it a Historical if it's a woman buyer, or a man who has expressed a dislike for "Westerns." Or if she says she only reads suspense, your book is suddenly a suspense, in a western setting. Cross genre lines, you may do us all some good.

Dress the part. They want to see a star, give them a star.

Don't be offended by anyone. Tell those who say they'll wait until it's in the library that you hope they do and to please read it when it arrives there, or those that want to wait to buy it in the used bookstore to make sure they tell their friends if they like it. Go on to the next live one. What you're doing, after all, is not just selling, but selling in order to spread the word and build your readership. So spread the word, even if you don't make a sale.

"I don't read that crap," is the worst you'll normally get by being assertive. You must then assume he's stupid because he probably doesn't read any crap, not only your crap. Or more likely that his hemorrhoids are flaring up--as yours will be if you sit there unmoving and un-selling for two hours.

Get a signing *partner* if you're so inclined. I sell a lot of books to ladies Kat stops, who don't read romance or romantic suspense; and she sells a lot of books to women (and even men) I stop, who'll buy for themselves or for mom or sis or grandma. But make sure you don't step on each other's closes.

Sell those books, and that two hours on a hard seat won't even be noticed.

And maybe, just maybe, you'll win a few faithful fans.

End of article.

As a result of that simple selling, we got lots of books on shelves where they might not have been otherwise, and made lots of friends of booksellers.

Now, it's millions of books later.

So, that's an example of simple selling at the lowest common denominator.

Was I going 'against the grain' in setting up my booksignings? You bet.

How many authors would drag the table, set up by the bookseller, from the back of the store to the front, when the bookseller had gone to a lot of work to place it there, with a nice vase of daisies. How many would say, "hey, we need some books on the table," or "hey, we need some books on the shelf, as well, as bashful buyers will pass by but want the book, and go into the shelves looking for it." How many would say, "Hey, I love chatting with you, but you want me to sell books, so let's chat after the booksigning is over."

All of those things, and more, are going 'against the grain.'

Along that same vein, never, never give up. Here's an example:

I wanted to try booksignings at military bases. I knew that most military bases had a base exchange where everything was sold, including books. Books, to such places, to supermarkets and to drug stores were, at the time, sold first to the store via independent book distrubutors. There were some 1,500 such ID's around the country.

On a hunch, I called the ID in a city near an Air Force Base and offered to go there and sign books at the base exchange. The reaction was, since I was not Stephen King or John Grisham, "Don't call us, we'll call you."

Okay, so much for that effort. However, not to be so easily dismissed, I called the base and asked for the base exchange, talked to the manager, who told me that all Army and Air Force base exchanges west of the Mississippi were operated by AAFE's, out of Dallas, Texas.

So I called AAFE's and found out who ran the place, then I signed a book and sent it off to him with the offer to sign books at his base exchanges. In one week he'd faxed every base exchange west of the Mississippi with my offer, and I was swamped, including a very sheepish call from the ID who'd been so rude. I couldn't help but respond, "I'll check my schedule and call you back." Childish and churlish, but I got some silent satisfaction therefrom.

"You don't get paid for the hour. You get paid for the value you bring to the hour." Jim Rohn

So 'Against The Grain?'

Back to real estate.

I quickly learned that real estate sales people are just like all sales people, in fact like almost all people.

When they get a little comfortable, they ease off. When they have something to do that's more fun than working, they ease off.

Going against the grain?   When Christmas comes along, everyone wants to get in the mood, slow down or quit working, go Christmas shopping. When I was selling houses, which I only did for a little more than a year, I found that the office got very, very lonely as Christmas approached. I did my Christmas shopping the week before, or asked my wife to do most of it, and hit the office early and stayed late. When those calls came in, and they did as someone in need of a place to live, and who might have been in a buying mood—with the Christmas spirit—was shopping for a house. I was there to sell them one while my good friends and co-workers were out Christmas shopping or at Christmas parties, taking advantage of all that Christmas cheer.

I didn't mind being a little late to the party.

And I'm not saying 'don't have a life.' I'm saying life is a lot easier and more fun when you're successful.

But the best example of going against the grain is when everyone is saying, "Oh, my God, business is sooooo bad."

Let's look back at 1985, the year I sold over one hundred million in real estate product.

Here's a quote directly from the FDIC webpage regarding 1985 and the years leading up to it:

December, 1982--Garn - St Germain Depository Institutions Act of 1982 enacted. This Reagan Administration initiative is designed to complete the process of giving expanded powers to federally chartered S&Ls and enables them to diversify their activities with the view of increasing profits. Major provisions include: elimination of deposit interest rate ceilings; elimination of the previous statutory limit on loan to value ratio; and expansion of the asset powers of federal S&Ls by permitting up to 40% of assets in commercial mortgages, up to 30% of assets in consumer loans, up to 10% of assets in commercial loans, and up to 10% of assets in commercial leases.

December, 1982--In response to the massive defections of state chartered S&Ls to the federal system, Nolan Bill passes in California. Allows California-chartered S&Ls to invest 100% of deposits in any kind of venture. Similar plans adopted in Texas and Florida.

1983--Lower market interest rates return many S&Ls to health. 35% of institutions, however, still sustain losses. 9% of all S&Ls (representing 10% of industry assets) are insolvent by GAAP standards.

March, 1983--Edwin Gray becomes Chairman of the Federal Home Loan Bank Board. Beginning in 1984 and continuing throughout his tenure, regulatory and supervisory measures passed by the Bank Board begin the reversing of deregulation.

November, 1983--Bank Board raises net worth requirement for newly chartered S&Ls to 7%.

March, 1984--Failure of Empire Savings of Mesquite, TX. "Land flips" and other criminal activities are a pattern at Empire. This failure would eventually cost the taxpayers approximately $300 million.

April, 1984--Bank Board moves jointly with the FDIC to attempt to eliminate deposit insurance for brokered deposits. Federal court rejects this attempt in mid-1984 as overstepping statutory limits.

July, 1984--Bank Board requires S&L management to adopt policies and procedures for managing interest rate risk.

January, 1985--Bank Board limits the amount of brokered deposits to 5% of deposits at FSLIC insured institutions failing to meet their net worth requirements. Bank Board also limits direct investment (equity securities, real estate, service corporations, and operating subsidiaries) to the greater of 10% of assets or twice the S&L's net worth, provided the institution meets regulatory net worth.

March, 1985--Ohio bank holiday. Anticipated failure of Home State Savings Bank of Cincinnati, OH and possible depletion of Ohio state deposit insurance fund cause Governor Celeste to close Ohio S&Ls. Eventually, those that can qualify for federal deposit insurance are allowed to reopen.

May, 1985--S&L failures in Maryland eventually cause loss to state deposit insurance fund and Maryland taxpayers of $185 million. Ohio and Maryland S&L failures helped kill state deposit insurance funds.

July, 1985--Chairman Gray begins transfer of federal examiners to the twelve regional Federal Home Loan Banks so that they are no longer overseen by OMB and their salaries are paid directly by the Bank Board system.

August, 1985--Only $4.6 billion in FSLIC insurance fund. Chairman Gray tries to gain support for recapitalizing FSLIC on Capitol Hill. In 1986, GAO estimates the loss to the insurance fund to be around $20 billion.

December, 1985--Bank Board allows S&L examiners to "classify" questionable loans and other assets for the purpose of requiring loan loss reserves.

So, what happened was that many savings and loans, and other financial institutions were, to risk the use of a colloquialism, on their butts.

Reagan had make the mistake of thinking that because a savings and loan executive was a very smart guy that he could expand the institutions profits by getting into the real estate development biz. Wrong!

Real estate development is a tough biz, and bean counters or execs who've come up through the ranks at savings and loans, many who started as tellers, do not real estate developers make. At least not necessarily so.

As savings and loans charged around real estate markets, trying to get into a business they had no real experience in, and using OPM (other people's money), they got into lots of bad investments, and got skinned by lots of real estate developers who were more than willing to take far greater risks with money invested by savings and loans than they would ever take with their own.

Joint ventures were rampant between real estate developers and savings and loans.

Suddenly, savings and loans were carrying thousands of failed developments on their books (while developers made huge profits in fees), and the regulators were saying, "Get rid of your R.E.O. or we'll close you down. R.E.O., for your information, is Real Estate Owned.

Most real estate brokers ran around yelling, "The sky is falling, the sky is falling," because savings and loans were going broke right and left, and not making those loans that had formerly been so easy to obtain.

So, again, against the grain. Look for opportunity, and opportunity in this particular instance was to 'save the day' for savings and loans. Help them get rid of their R.E.O., be a hero, and collect fat commissions along the way.

Savings and loans might be out of the loan market, but only when it came to new ventures. They were more than willing to make loans so long as those loans were tied to the disposition of their R.E.O. and helped them stay in business by getting that product off their books. In fact, they were both anxious and eager to makes those loans. Far more so than ever before.

While the average real estate broker either stayed home, or tried to sell those failed developments for the savings and loans (generally a real uphill battle), I worked to find folks who needed loans, and would buy properties in return for getting same.

Quid pro quo was the order of the day.

And I made well over one hundred million dollars in sales and negotiated many huge real estate loans, for fees, as a result.

Savings and loans not only got rid of their R.E.O., but they made new loans and breathed new life into their institutions. Some of those deals worked out, some did not, but all gave the institutions more time to solve their problems.

While others saw catastrophe, I saw opportunity.

Always, always, always look for opportunity by going against the grain.

The Publishing Biz

After enjoying writing for a living and promoting my wife's writing career for many years, along came another radical change in the publishing business, and consequently in my business life. The internet. At first I was very skeptical about selling books over the internet. Being one, like many other old farts, set in their ways, I wanted a book in hand. I enjoyed the feel and even the smell of a printed book. However I soon succumbed as I watched the market in so-called eBooks grow.

So, I learned how to format and upload my own books. I had written some 35 or more at the time. I'd had success with those hard to penetrate New York publishing houses, unlike the millions of books submitted that languor on publishing house bookshelves never examined, or now in hyperspace as digital files never opened. And much of that was due to my willingness to sell. The average reclusive writer would never consider picking up the phone and calling an acquiring editor in some twenty-story high edifice, New York publishing house. I had no problem doing so, or sticking my paw out at some writer's conference and introducing myself to an editor or publisher there to give the keynote address.

But, to be truthful, after more than twenty books with three different New York publishers, I was tired of having to explain western lexicon to folks who'd never been over the Hudson River. So, I jumped on the opportunity to publish myself.

But I soon realized I was in the same position I had been when I started in the Real Estate biz. I didn't know how to sell. Oh, yeah, I was great at face-to-face selling, but over the internet? It was a whole new world.

Luckily an old friend sent me an email. I was doing a political blog and he said he could increase my audience. And would do so for free as he liked my message.

My audience went up ten-fold as he was an SEO (search engine optimization) expert. He'd been selling on the web for many years. Soon, my audience had increased ten-fold. And, it dawned on me, could he sell books?

I've never been greedy when it came to sharing as I long ago learned that half of something was way better than all of nothing. So, I made him an offer: I'll put up my 35 books, to which I had rights returned, and would split 50/50 anything we would earn if he'd take on the job of selling them on the web.

And it wasn't long before I was making twenty times what I'd been making, after splitting with him. I knew something about writing. He knew how to sell on the web.

Then came another epiphany. I knew lots of other writers, many of them my age, who had lots of books in their backlist. Books which had "run their course" and rights had been returned to the author from those New York publishers. I ran into one old friend at a Western Writer's of America conference. A writer I much admired who was in his eighth decade and who had nearly three hundred books in his backlist. Yes, that's three hundred. And I liked and admired him and he confided he hadn't made a buck off his writing for nearly ten years.

A travesty.

I wrote in more than one genre but enjoyed writing westerns. As it came to pass, most NY publishers were abandoning the western as sales had fallen. I realized, what was a smidgen to a NY publisher with hundreds of employees might be a boon to a couple of old country boys. As I had with my new partner, I suggested to this old friend: "You have lots of books in your backlist. How about letting us try and sell a few and we'll split what we make with you?"

That was the beginning of a company, Wolfpack Publishing. A company that in four years had thirty-five authors and over four hundred books published on the internet and in paper (now many more authors and books). We were the 4th largest western publisher in the USA, working out of our respective homes with three independent contractors…no employees.

That's called going against the grain. I heard time and time again, the western was dead. However, westerns, as are historicals, are never untimely. They are written in, say, 1870, so one's not wondering why the protagonist didn't Google to get an answer. They are always topical, for their time and place.

I reached the age of seventy-five and decided, again, I didn't want to work that hard, nor did I want to worry about lots of old friends we were publishing. By the way, when I sold out to my partner, I was sending monthly checks of ten grand to that old friend who'd trusted us with his life's work.

I'm very proud of that.

"You are what you think. You are what you go for. You are what you do." Bob Richards

L. J. Martin

Bonus Section

L. J. Martin

Who is the boss?

Let's see…is it the guy who owns the company? Is it the company president? Is it the department manager? Is it your immediate shift manager? Is it the guy or gal who signs your check?

You'll soon learn it's none of those.

And, right after that mysterious 'who,' it's you who are the most important cog in the business wheel.

This may come as a surprise to you, but YOU are the foundation of your company, and other than the customer, the most important screw or bolt which holds the whole bridge together.

A recent morning's example is typical of what's happening in the country.

The hotel dinning room opens at 6:00 AM, or so says the front desk.

What a surprise, no one in the dinning room; clanking coming from the kitchen. If I was truly in a hurry I would have wandered into the kitchen and shouted out, "is anyone awake?" But rather I found a booth, seated myself, and went to work on my laptop. After ten minutes I would have come to a slow boil (no morning coffee = grumpy), but I realized there was free coffee in the lobby, so I fetched a cup and was content until 6:15 when the lady showed up with an "I had some prep to do." Being an old fashioned boy, I presume the prep would be done BEFORE opening…which is why it's called, "prep." As I was in North Dakota when this happened, I was not shocked to receive a seemingly sincere apology from the lady. Had I been in California….

Later that day my wife witnessed the same waitress try to seat two different pairs of customers at the same table so she wouldn't have to open another section farther from the kitchen…one of those pairs, obviously having private matters to discuss, huffed away. Lost business, lost revenue, a business just that much closer to closing its doors and throwing two or three dozen folks out of jobs.

To show that I'm not merely a grumpy old fart, I'm happy to report that the following morning, same time, I wandered into the same booth, waited only one minute and while sliding out of my booth to go to the lobby to fetch my own coffee, a very pleasant young lady hurried out of the kitchen and made me feel very welcome. She was not only efficient but when another old fart wandered in and with mouth gaping and turned so far down his false teeth were about to tumble out over his receding chin, ordered a dry bagel and immediately asked very nastily if they charged extra for a pad of butter and a dollop of jelly, then unsatisfied that he hadn't ruined her morning, asked, "so I suppose you charge for the water?" To my utter surprise and satisfaction the young woman was pleasant no matter how much black paint he tried to pour in her bucket, killing him with kindness.

I later suggested to the restaurant manager that she get a raise.

What got me started on this particular rant?

I think America needs to get back to work, and to do it with the same attention to detail many, most who were successful, did while I was growing up. And all they need to do is to recognize who's the boss in a free enterprise society.

At the risk of not being politically correct...something I've never been accused of: One of America's most well run states is Utah. My wife and I drive the length of Utah at least once a year on our way from Spring-Summer-Fall residence in Montana to Winter in California. Utah takes care of business, maybe it's the wonderful work ethic of the Mormons, but when you go into a gas station mini-market run by some Pakistani gentleman and his wife and four kids, to your great surprise you'll find the restroom open and CLEAN. In California all restrooms in those establishments are strangely out of order. Yes, I know I'm being politically incorrect, however: Pakistani = Out Of Order Restroom. Which is probably just as well as the one out of ten thousand who might be admitted to one reputed be in working order find it to be filthy, and you'd be better off to climb in the half-full dumpster out back of the place to do your business. But I digress....

You who are the most important cog in the business wheel!

L. J. Martin

Attitude Is Everything!

On one of those recent drives south we stopped at a combination gas station mini-market, and in the market was one of those chain burger joints, or a small version thereof. I seldom waste the calories on fast food, but we were in a hurry, so I approached the counter, the single customer in the place. A young man, hefty in size (saying "fat" is not politically correct), wandered out of the small kitchen area and approached the counter. His bill cap was not turned backward, to his credit, but was pulled so low over his eyes they couldn't be seen, only half his nose, his pursed lips, and both his chins. Even though I was in a hurry, I decided to have a little fun. He approached the counter, eyes unseen, and took up a position across the counter from me, ...and said absolutely nothing. No "hello," no "welcome to WalMart," no "may I help you,"...nothing. Sooooo, I said nothing. Having been a salesman most of my life (and a damn good one, I might add) I know the value of silence. Dead, penetrating, attention getting, eventually very irritating, silence. Finally, when I refused to break the silence, he began to fidget, and eventually (I guess he was afraid I was either voice impaired or was about to pull a gat and hold the place up) he raised his cap, stepped back, and eyeballed me, his gaze very suspicious. I managed to keep a straight face, even though I wanted to break out laughing, but rather I gave him as hard a look as I could muster.

Finally, he managed, "You want something?"

I couldn't help myself, "No, I just came in to stare at you over the counter and see how long it would take to try and discover if I was a customer."

That, as I might have suspected, was greeted with a, "Uh?"

So, I ordered. And watched very carefully to make sure he didn't do something obscene to the food. He did glance over his shoulder several times to make sure this obviously insane old man didn't vault the counter and execute a rear attack.

And now, almost every time I deal with a counter person, I notice how poorly trained most counter people (supposedly sales people) are in this free enterprise country of ours, and to decide to try and do my very small part to try and show them the error of their ways, and make them aware of who's the boss in this great country of ours, and why that concept, observed by past generations, has made her the great country she's become.

Let me suggest to you that success, no matter how small a success one incident might seem to you, is one of life's greatest pleasures. It's one of the things that makes getting up in the morning a pleasure rather than a chore; it's a precursor to mental and physical health, it's the essence of a happy existence. It makes work a pleasure.

So, let's investigate a few ways to accomplish that goal, and why we should.

Why should you, as a counter person or sales person, maybe making minimum wage, give a damn who the boss might be?

If you haven't surmised the answer to that simple question as of yet, the customer is the boss.

The customer is boss.

The customer is BOSS!

L. J. Martin

What Good Are Customers Anyway!

Please consider that all the money any business accumulates, or doesn't, comes from the customer. It doesn't matter if it's a good or service your selling, the customer is the boss, and if the customer is unhappy, and no longer shows up to buy your good or service, there will be no more money; no more counter person, no more shift manager, no more general manager, no more vice president, no more company president, nor board of directors nor chairman of the board. And that sad process all begins with you and your relationship with the customer.

As said in nearly the first sentence, you are the foundation of your company, and other than the customer, the most important screw or bolt that holds the whole bridge together.

And therein lies the reason that government is perverse. No matter how good, or how poor, the service offered, the check still arrives at the end of the month. It's the one instance in our economy where the customer is not the boss, at least now in the eyes of the service provider. It's far to far to reach to understand that his or her paycheck originates with the taxpayer. Not that there are not some excellent government employees, some with some personal pride it what they do, but by the nature of "no profit necessary," they are few and far between.

It's not only your company that depends upon you, but think of the suppliers who count on your company's business, on the other employees who depend upon your company for their jobs…for those weekly or monthly checks that pay their rent or house payment and keep their kids in shoes and lunch money. And the landlord who owns the building or buildings your company rents…and the chain goes on and on and on.

Suddenly, you should realize how important you are.

So, don't let them down, and more importantly, don't let yourself down. Sure, you might find another job, not so easy as it once was, but they are still out there. But if your company fails, you've failed to a certain extent, and, trust me, you don't want to get in the habit of failing. It's bad for both your mental and physical health.

What can you do to help insure your company's health, and success?

Easy, remember that each and every customer is the boss. Is that any easy chore? Usually it is, however, many times it's not. As I pointed out in the introduction to this book, some customers are tougher than others. Some are downright obnoxious, and those are the ones who'll test your resolve to make sure your company is successful.

You must approach every customer with an open mind, you must have no preconceived notions about that man or woman across the counter. Don't judge. You don't know, for instance, that he or she was not informed that morning that they had terminal cancer. Would you be less than bubbly under that circumstance? Her mother may have died that morning. Or even merely her cat or his dog (more important than mother to some in this perverted society we've created). Or it may simply be that they've run out of money and this hamburger you're selling may be the last meal they can afford until day after tomorrow when they get paid again.

Or they may be one of the very few human beings who's just a smartass or who believes that every glass is half empty rather than half full.

But you'll never know which customer is which, or why they have the attitude that makes you want to give them less than stellar service.

Your job, one you've chosen to take money to perform, is a trust. It's a trust given to you by your employer, and he, and a lot of others are depending upon you.

Your job is a TRUST!

Prove Yourself Worthy

I've never had a book, booklet, pamphlet, or manual, whatever this turns out to be, that had so much material so easily accessed as this "who's the boss." All I have to do is walk into almost any business and I'm confronted with material.

Only yesterday, needing a haircut, I called my local beauty shop (boy do I miss barber shops) and made an appointment for 10:30 AM, the earliest she said I could get in. I showed up at 10:05 and the girl was alone in the shop, sitting behind the greeting counter, reading a magazine. I asked, hopefully, if I could get in early. "No," she said, "I have a ten o'clock." I glanced at the time, now 10:07. What she should have said is "I have a ten o'clock, and I try and wait ten minutes to give my customers a break, but if she's not here by 10:10, I'll be happy take you early and she can take your 10:30." I don't have a lot of hair and I'm a fifteen-minute cut, at the most. And a customer who's late should expect to "lose their turn."

But she didn't say that.

I will tell you that I'm never late. It's my belief that folk's time is important, and if you're habitually late, what you're saying is "my time is more important than yours," or, otherwise, "I'm more important that you are." I find it offensive to be late, and only tolerate it in others for a short time.

I walked across the street to grab some breakfast, as I had yet to do so. I rise really early, coffee it up, and usually try and have brunch so I limit the intake to two meals a day.

My morning continued to be more material for "who's the boss."

The place was fairly busy, two waitresses for about twenty people. It's a great breakfast for $5.00, two eggs, bacon or sausage, spuds, and toast, as their intent is to draw in customers for the casino in the next room. I climbed up to the counter and ordered, asking if I could get quick service as I had to be out of there in 25 minutes. To the girls credit she said, "maybe, but we're really busy." However, as she was honest, I said, "great, coffee to start." I waited for a few minutes, and counted, as she picked up the coffee pot and filled those already served four separate times, passing my upturned cup each time. I was six feet from the coffee pot, with an upturned cup waiting, shouting out for attention. I finally walked into the casino section (in Montana half the bars and restaurants have casinos) and offer free coffee while you pump your quarters into the machine. I filled up my own and returned to the counter.

To their credit, I was served quickly. I immediately pulled out my credit card and said "I'd like to pay." Which was ignored. I was also three feet from the register. Another waitress worked the register and I asked her, "May I pay," and she replied, "I'll get your server." As all I had was a twenty dollar bill, I quickly asked, as she had the register open, "May I have change?" To which she replied, "You bet, in a moment," but closed the register and walked away.

I sensed a miffed waitress who was not about to help another waitress…to the distress of her customer, to the distress of her company, and to be factual, to her own distress but she was not smart enough to know it. No, she was not my waitress, however any customer in the house is the customer of each and every employee, and if that customer is given reason not to return, then all suffer.

I finished my breakfast and caught my "server," a term I was beginning to believe a misnomer, and asked, "May I pay." She said, "you bet," and informed me it was "three bucks…opp's, five bucks including the coffee." She then looked down her nose at me as if I'd committed a crime by going next door and filling my own coffee cup.

She didn't mention that the coffee was free in the next room, and she had no idea that I hadn't come into the restaurant from the casino in the first instance. I made no complaint, however, I made no something else as well, that something else was a tip.

Yesterday was the first time in twenty years that I have not left a tip. It's been my rule to tip ten percent for lousy service, fifteen percent for average service, and twenty percent or slightly more for good service. Upon rare occasion for excellent service, over and above, I've tipped way more. It doesn't have to be excellent service to get twenty percent, just good service. I figure the Good Lord has been good to me, and I like to pass a little along. But not yesterday.

And the young lady in the hair salon did not get off to the best second-start, as I entered at exactly 10:30, my appointment time, she was talking on the phone, obviously a personal call. She'd already demonstrated that her magazine was more important than her customer, now she was making sure I knew that her phone call was more important.

A person who realized who the boss was would have terminated the call when she saw me coming, which was easy as there's glass all across the front of the salon, and I'd seen her see me before I reached the door. Nope, four or five sentences later, she said, "I've got to go," with a tone that indicated she had to take care of a pesky customer.

I would have waited another three or four sentences before I excused myself without a tip of the hat, and most certainly without a tip, but she terminated the call.

I did redeem myself with the hair stylist (who's ten o'clock never showed, by the way) and tipped her (fifteen percent) as she gave me an excellent haircut, if not intelligent service.

The crux of this article is your customer owes you nothing, he owes your business nothing, unless you're unique in what you offer, he can easily go elsewhere

Nothing!

You owe him/her everything.

You would not receive a paycheck were it not for your customer. Your company's landlord, suppliers, vendors, and others who depend upon some payment from your company/business, would not be paid, and consequently their suppliers, etc., and employees, would not be paid, were it not for your customer.

The customer is the boss; a truism, ultimate, final, without question.

If you're wise, you'll not expect to be given the benefit of the doubt by your customer, and you'll always extend that courtesy to him

He, after all, is the boss.

The customer owes you NOTHING, you Owe him everything!

Self-Worth Begins With Honesty!

When I was six I was in what was then called a five and dime store. Probably the closest equivalent now would be the dollar store. I helped myself to an eraser. On returning to the car, my mother spotted the eraser in my hand. She promptly led me back into the store and had me not only return the eraser to the proprietor, but apologize, then to my great dismay, asked the gentleman behind the counter if he had a broom. He did, and she handed it to me and said "sweep the floor. I'll be back to check on you." With the proprietor exclaiming that sweeping was not necessary, he was promptly and decisively corrected by my mother, and I spent a couple of hours learning the error of my way.

Too bad today's mothers are not so astute, and today's businesses are not so fearful of being sued that they'd never let a six year old work in their aisle.

It was however a lesson long remembered.

When you work for someone, who benefits most from your being an absolute honest employee? Were you to take an ice cream cone from a successful mini-market where you worked, would it break the place? Of course not. If you took a box of pencils or file folders home from the office for your personal use, would it break the lawyers or doctors for whom you work. Of course not.

So, what's the harm of a little dishonesty?

You by now know how I like adages and proverbs. The one most applicable here is an age old one: the rotten apple spoils the barrel. When other employees see you habitually come in late (stealing time is stealing money), or taking extra time at your coffee break, or taking a book into the restroom and spending thirty minutes doing what should take five, then you are the rotten apple in the barrel.

But more importantly than your actions are as an influence on others, it's the lesson you're teaching yourself.

Getting away with something illegal, immoral, dishonest becomes a habit that will eventually crush the sprit and the soul. Some have said it far better:

"Whoever is careless with the truth in small matters cannot be trusted with important matters" -- Albert Einstein

"Honesty is the first chapter of the book of wisdom." -- Thomas Jefferson

"Living a lie will reduce you to one." –Ashly Lorenzana

"No legacy is so rich as honesty." –William Shakespeare

"Honesty is the first chapter of the book of wisdom."

--Thomas Jefferson

Make It Easy On The Customer!

California seems to be the end of the earth when it comes to customer service…and most service employees might as well jump off the edge for all the good they are.

A simple question: Do you think you're more important to your place of employment than are your customers?

If you do, you're dead wrong.

I took an early ride with my cameras down to the harbor to take some pictures of the pelicans, which were working a bait spawn and from sixty feet in the air, doing their dive bomber act. As the morning drew on I drove to a small 20 seat café near the end of the harbor drive, one I'd read a recent review about in the local paper.

It opened at 7:00 AM and I was a few minutes early. There was only one car in the lot, and it was parked several parking spaces away, but I noticed a man behind the counter working, and he noticed me standing at the door.

Were I that man, whom I later found to be the manager or owner, with one customer standing outside, I would have opened five minutes early, if for no other reason than to allow my customer in out of the cold ocean breeze…and more so to make him feel welcome and even more so to make sure he didn't walk away. He did not come to the door, and even though there was another café a half-mile away and on my way home, I waited. At 7:00 he opened and had the coffee ready. I ordered, and before my order was up, a nice looking young lady came in, walked behind the counter, and put on an apron. Obviously she was a waitress. I had ordered, so I wasn't particularly offended that she didn't bother to greet me or come over to see if I needed anything.

I had parked in a place closest to the walkway to the café, in a lot with one hundred parking places. I would guess the parking lot seldom fills, however, the young lady parked next to me, nearest the walkway.

Why's that of interest?

Because the next few cars might have filled at least that first row, and then the next customer might have been handicapped or wearing a cast from his trip to the ski hill, and because he had an extra forty feet to walk, might have gone to the café down the road, where the employees were smart enough to park in the spaces far from the entrance, and leave the near spaces to the "boss," the customer.

As a young man I was impressed by a story I read about an executive who'd just taken over Avis, then the number two car rental company in the country.

His executives, on the second day of his taking over, were surprised to arrive at the office and find their names had been painted out, removed from the curb that formerly fronted their "private" spaces.

Fearing they'd been fired, each of them inquired of him "why?"

He replied, "Did you notice my car was near the front door? If so, you should note it was because I was the first one in the office this morning. If you want a place near the door, beat the rest of the employees to work."

I love that story. A great manager is one who leads by example. To quote an old adage, "It ain't what you say, it's what you do."

It ain't what you say, it's what you do!

Let A Smile Be Your Umbrella!

Do you enjoy being smiled at? Isn't a smile actually a symbol of approval? Do you enjoy being approved?

I've often heard that it takes more muscles to frown than it does to smile. Research tells me that's not necessarily so. It ain't necessarily so, to quote another line from a song, as is the title to this section. So you don't smile just because it's easier. You smile because it's way, way better than a frown for your business, and consequently for your job, and believe it or not, for your health.

A smile protects your job, just as an umbrella protects you from getting wet.

You're not getting a smile from the customer, so why bother to give him one? Do you remember that customer who just found out he had terminal cancer? Do you think a smile is too much to offer him, even if the corners of his mouth are turned sharply down?

Want to know something else?

A smile is good for YOU, not only for the person who's seeing you smile.

Guess what? For a long while scientists have known that emotions are reflected by changes in the body. If you're happy, you smile. And guess what, it works both ways. If you smile, you get more and more happy. Do you want to be happy? If you don't, you need some help that I can't give you in this book.

Smiling to make yourself happy was first called the "facial feedback hypothesis." So, let's give it a try.

Smile. I mean it, smile right now.

Sometimes the conscious effort of making yourself smile actually amuses you, and not only do you smile, but you giggle, if you're prone to giggling. I flat out guarantee you that if you smiled when I suggested it, you not only felt happier, but you'll enjoy this book far more. That's the emotional effect of the physical act of smiling. In fact, you'll enjoy life a lot more.

There were actually experiments conducted to demonstrate the psychology of the smile. In the late 80's researchers had subjects hold a pencil in their mouths in different ways while judging cartoons, telling the subjects the test was about emotion, when in fact it was about the effect of flexing certain facial muscles upon emotion. Those who held the pencil crossways, making the face use the same muscles as used in a smile, judged the cartoons much more funny than those instructed to hold the pencil in other ways.

In a later study subjects were told to judge printed images, while "lifting their cheeks" which forced them to use the smile muscles, or to "furrow their brow" which forced the use of the frown muscles. The "lift your cheeks" group found the images much more pleasant that the "furrow your brow" subjects.

It's no surprise to me.

Smile and the world smiles with you, frown and you're likely to frown alone.

We all love to smile, and your customers love to see you smile, and will be happier, and will likely judge what you're selling them, be it donuts or Duisenberg's, much more pleasant.

L. J. Martin

Smile, it makes YOU happy!

So, What Do You Want To Be?

I ask the question because it's important. What do you want to be, who do you want to be? It's important to your company, and sure as heck should be important to you.

The fact is you control who and what you want to be, and it all starts with attitude, and attitude is partially controlled by that simple act of smiling. And beyond that, attitude is most-certainly controlled by self-satisfaction, which is, or should be, the realization that you're doing a good job…a great job…and your hard work is appreciated. Another old adage, the last one: You can satisfy some of the people all of the time, and all of the people some of the time, but you can't satisfy all of the people all of the time.

But you can satisfy yourself that you're doing your very best to do so.

And you should, if success is your goal.

In closing let me quote a gentleman who came from Russia as a teenager, destitute, and became the owner and operator of one of the country's largest cattle, sheep and meat packing operations. Oscar Rudnick was fond of saying, "The customer is not always right, the customer is not always wrong…but the customer is always the customer."

I don't know how it could be better said.

I wrote this for young people just trying their wings in business, but all of us might glean a thing or two. Unlike the first section, this is first person.

The Joy of the Journey

By L. J. Martin

LIFE

Is Straight Ahead

A Primer for The Young

(and maybe you too)

Yogi Berra, one of baseball's great catcher's, and later a manager, of the New York Yankees said many fascinating things. Among the most thought provoking: "If you come to a fork in the road, take it."

And, if you, young man or lady, come to a fork in the road "take it," as either way can lead you to a successful, happy, and fulfilling life if you go about your journey with the proper attitude and obey a few very basic rules. You see, it doesn't matter what you set out to do, so long as it's an honorable pursuit, as the joy of the journey is not only in arriving, but in the journey itself.

It's the people you meet along the way, the things you learn, and the friends you make. That's the joy of the journey. But the journey can also be a nightmare. 99.99% of the time it's totally up to you. There will be things that happen to you along the way, rocks in the road, and how you react to them makes a big difference…joy or misguided justification.

So, what's misguided justification? It's merely the excuse you make for losing or messing up. If it's always someone else's fault then you're on a path to failure. Some things can't be avoided, but all things are a learning experience and can usually be avoided the next time. And by far most errors you make in life are the fault of only one person…you.

If I have one regret it's not keeping a journal and recording the friends I've made along this journey of mine. Friends made, then forgotten because of the ravages of time. A lousy excuse, the ravages of time. The real reason is my inattention to doing what I now wish I'd done, and that's keep a record…a journal or diary. There must be a thousand people I owe, who

I'd like to drop a note and say thanks for past favors. But they weren't noted, and it's a frustration that follows me, and occasionally haunts me if I can't remember a name to tie to a kindness, or even a laugh. Or a person I might visit or even call for advice about where to visit in their home town. A friend or even casual acquaintance is better than a visitor's bureau, a chamber of commerce, or a guidebook.

One of the first things you should learn as you set out on your journey: Forget the favors you do others; never forget the favors they do you. If you loan someone money, forget it. If they loan you money put repayment on the list right after breathing. It's a matter of character and character is the fuel that fires your successful and fulfilling journey.

Most of the things that define character are super simple. Most choices in life are just that: simple. Here's a very important, super simple one, that should be on top your list: It's not what you say…it's what you do. You'll find that talk is truly cheap. If you tell a friend you'll be there, then be there, hell or high water. If you don't do what you say you'll do—even something as simple as telling a friend "I'll be there"—always remember that your friend is counting on you and may have, probably did, set aside something else he or she could have done. Probably rearranged his or her schedule because you said, "I'll be there." What's so important about doing what you say? If you don't, if you cause someone to change their schedule or wait for you and if you don't show up, you're saying, "I'm more important that you are." If you want to lose friends, if you want to be disliked, go through life saying, "I'm more important than you are." And it doesn't have to be stated verbally. Remember, it's not what you say, it's what you do. At the least, call as soon as you know you won't make it. In these days of cell phones, unless you're hit by a truck, there's little excuse for not calling. Humility, good sense, and common courtesy never cost anyone a friend. And as you move along on your journey you'll find you treasure your friends more and more.

Another character defining trait is finishing what you start. Leaving a job undone is an insult to you and the job, be it washing a car, mowing the lawn, or doing what your boss asks you to do. As an employee, it's critical you finish what you start. If self-employed it can mean paying the rent or house payment, or not. And that can mean a home…or becoming homeless. A job only 99% complete is not a job "almost finished" or a job "nearly finished"…it's a job unfinished. What you're saying by what you do, or don't do, not by what you say, is that the job isn't WORTH doing. And if you're employed, and your boss thinks you don't think a job assigned you is worth doing, it means to him you don't value your job and he'll likely look for someone who will. You "didn't finish" is worse than coming in 2nd, and remember, 2nd is the first loser.

As you read this if you look back and say, "I haven't formed any of these habits and it's too late now," then remember another adage, "Today is the first day of the rest of your life."

You've heard all these admonitions before and maybe so much you think them clichés, but like stereotypes, clichés became clichés and stereotypes came to be stereotypes, because they were proclaimed so often, not because they are necessarily wrong. In fact, normally because they were so right.

And success? Success is merely a way of keeping score regarding how well you've done on the journey. Success can be measured in many ways. How many folks have you made smile? And I don't mean by telling the joke of the day. Made smile by making their task, their life, easier and more rewarding? By being on time? By complimenting even when you know it's a stretch of the truth. By doing a good job and pleasing your friend, your girl- or boyfriend, your spouse, your instructor, or your boss. And it can be measured monetarily, but that's only part of the equation. To be truthful, your success makes you smile, and other's want to be around someone who smiles, not a sad sack who's unhappy with self, who's continually frowning.

So, smile.

Make acceptance a simple matter. A person smiling is much easier to accept than one frowning, unless a smile is inappropriate in the situation. If someone tells you their favorite pet had to be put down, a smile is inappropriate. Your appearance and grooming is important to acceptance. It's easy to show what a rebel you are by piercing your tongue or nose or a nipple, or tattooing a black widow on your neck, but it doesn't endear you to most employers, or educators, or normally to your parents or grandparents. Why make the journey more difficult? If you want a butterfly or black widow with you always, then put it on a butt cheek where a job interviewer won't see it…and if he or she asks to check out that cheek, run.

Cleanliness almost goes without saying. Have you gone in a fast food joint and had the counter person walk up with filthy hands? Are you going to eat what he serves? Is an employer going to hire or fire a person who runs business off? Use your head, then use your hands, soap, a comb, and a washing machine to clean your clothes and if you don't have one available wash that tee shirt and your sox in a service station bathroom lavatory.

Sometimes the hardest thing in life is knowing which bridge to cross and which to burn. But cleanliness and being presentable is an easy bridge to cross when you know acceptance is on the other side. And I don't mean you must get chapped lips kissing butt—someone else's butterfly or black widow—but using common sense and knowing what will or will not get you ahead is paving with gold what could be a rocky road.

There will be no journey and no joy if you're not a survivor. Some laws may not make much sense to you but most were enacted for good reason. Seat-belts are a good example. Wear your seat-belts and survive a simple roll over, don't and very likely have your pretty head squashed by that car you love so much. A statistic once proclaimed the easiest way to extend your life expectancy by 20 years was simply to hook up—and I don't mean as in the parlance of the day. Almost every week in our local paper and thousands of times across the country we get a report of an accident where a driver and/or passenger dies in a simple roll-over…no seatbelt worn. I can't help but say, "…died of stupidity."

There's no question while on your journey you'll be offered a toke or a snort. I know Miss Mary Jane is now legal in many states and I know all the arguments that it's no worse than Jack Daniels. I also know that a hooter stays with you for a month and alcohol is expelled by your body in one day—yeah, it kills some brain cells but we only use 10% of that organ if the researchers are right. So, I know that the results of smoking are cumulative, as crud builds up in your system. I limit my dope to a couple of 4 oz. glasses of red wine AFTER WORK, and would likely be much better off being a teetotaler. They call it dope for a reason and, yes, it lessens your resistance and contracts your common sense making it lots easier to try something harder, even a needle. Stupid, stupid, stupid, and a survivor wouldn't kowtow to that first temptation no matter how much peer pressure was heaped on…and it's not a friend who'd try and pull you over to the dark side. This is a tough enough world without trying to face it with diminished capability. That's damn foolish …particularly when a small error while all your good sense has flown to the wind can cost you your freedom or even your very life.

Dope is called dope for a very good reason. Don't be a dope.

Education, in any form, makes your life much easier. All you have to do is research the difference in income between the average high school dropout, high school graduate, college graduate, and masters and doctorate achievers to see the value of education. Sure, some folks make it fine without that college sheepskin, but again, why not play the odds? And your college days can be among the most fun, most challenging, and most satisfying of those on your journey. And education doesn't stop with school or university. A thinking person tries to learn something new every day, even days enjoyed in the 8th and 9th decade of their journey.

Parents! Parents love you which is one of the great advantages in life…and also can be a detriment at times. Parents' love is generally not tough love most times and there are many times when we, particularly as youngsters, need tough love. Parents who do not practice tough love are cowardly…they don't want to be hurt by your failures. They are not brave enough to expose you to that wicked world and make you make your own way.

If your parents don't punish you when you've done something wrong, and severely when you've done something severely wrong, you'll be both surprised and confused when you're punished by your instructor, your boss, and even your peers when later you screw up. Or worse, the law. And you will screw up…we all do.

And parents aren't perfect in other ways by any means. They can set a bad example as well as a good one. Because your parents drink, or toke, or snort doesn't make it right nor give you the excuse to be stupid. Set your own goals, and do the smart thing to accomplish them no matter the example set by family, friends, educators and others whose path you'll cross. I personally believe we should line up and piss on Dr. Spock's grave daily, as he's the one who started the trend of no corporal punishment for children. A slap on the butt for misbehavior while young is much easier to take, and as constructive, as being fired from a job later in life. That said punishment of children must be dealt with common sense and not in anger…as maddening as they (you) can be at times.

Health is a great gift, the most valuable you'll ever receive. Most of us, particularly the young, take it for granted. Protect it, value it, as if you've discovered a diamond mine for it's far more valuable than even that. Some, even the young, have discovered they can't take another step of life's journey as they've lost it. You must pay attention to what your body tells you. If you mistreat your body, it'll get even. I'm not telling you not to enjoy your life, not to get out on that ten-degree freezing ski slope and charge downhill, but use your head. If you discover a lump under your arm, and it stays there an extended time, it's time to have an expert take a look. Most of us hate hospitals and doctors…at least going to them…but time is the friend of many diseases and if they have time to get a hold on your soul, it's your fault. As a two-time cancer survivor who's busted lots of parts on the ol' bod, I can tell you it's important to be assertive about your health. It's your health, your body, and no one should pay as much attention as do you. This holds true from toes to teeth. And particularly for that gray matter between your ears. Don't ever discount that so called old cliché, "Laughter is the best medicine." It truly is. Stay well. Physically and mentally.

Courtesy and manners will get you places that a fancy car, expensive clothes, jewelry, and even many friends, will not. Learn manners, no matter the vogue of the time, and no matter what many women of today think, or parrot (pay attention girls), deep down from instincts developed when man was chasing mammoths and dodging saber tooth tigers, women want to be respected and cared for, by a man. If they resent a man opening a door for them, they're living in a dream world. I open doors for ladies, for older men, for folks with disabilities, and 99.99% of them see it as what it is, a sign of respect. I've known many young women who've said "I'm equal to any man." And, yes, they are, mentally, but very few are physically, all other things being equal. Treasure what God or evolution or whatever you believe in has bestowed upon mankind (okay, humankind). Love yourself for what and who you are and your journey will be much more fun, more appreciated, and likely more profitable. All that said, women and men should be equally valued in your eyes and the eyes of others...and if others don't, they're not only not worth your time, they're worth your scorn.

This is merely a paper, a short essay, written with my grandchildren in mind. A paper which I plan to turn into a book as there's lots more to making the journey. A book which I hope will be of benefit to all who set out on that grandest of all journey's…life.

Live it, love it…and make the very most of it.

L. J. Martin Bio

L. J. Martin is the author of 56 works of both fiction and non-fiction from Bantam, Avon, Pinnacle, Wolfpack Publishing, and Wolfpack Productions. He's formerly a publisher of over 400 titles from other authors as Wolfpack Publishing and currently publishing classroom instructional game books as Buttonwillow Book. He lives in Montana with his wife, NYT bestselling romantic suspense author Kat Martin and winters in Prescott, Arizona. He's been a horse wrangler, cook as both avocation and vocation, volunteer firefighter, real estate broker, general contractor, appraiser, disaster evaluator for FEMA, author, publisher and has traveled a good part of the world, some in his own ketch. A hunter, fisherman, photographer, cook, father and grandfather, he's been car and plane wrecked, and survived cancer twice. He carries a bail-enforcement, bounty hunter, shield. +His work has topped the Amazon genre lists in Action Adventure and Western. Join him on www.ljmartin.com. He has over 120 videos posted on

YouTube, with over a million views, edited by him on Final Cut Pro: search ljmartinwolfpack. You can join him at facebook.com/ljmartinauthor, on twitter at @westwrite, and on other social media sites. His Wolfpack Publishing LLC, now sold to a former partner, had great success in eBooks, having a disproportionate share of top action adventure novels in that genre, consistently over 60% of all of Amazon's classic western bestseller list during his tenure.

In case you enjoy reading…. Join me on www.ljmartin.com and sign up for the occasional email. My curriculum vitae:

Westerns:
Against the 7th Flag
Blackjack Brannigan
Blood Mountain
Buckshot
Condor Canyon
El Lazo
Eye for Eye
McCreed's Law
McKeag's Mountain
Mojave Showdown
Mr. Pettigrew
Nemesis
O' Rourke's Revenge
Revenge of the Damned
Rugged Trails
Shadow of the Grizzly
Shadows of Nemesis
Stranahan
The Benicia Belle
The Devil's Bounty
Tin Angel (Western Romance Written With Kat Martin)
Two Thousand Grueling Miles

West of the War
Wolf Mountain

Historicals:
Rush to Destiny
Shadow of the Mast

Action-Adventure, Crime & Thrillers:
Bullet Blues
Crimson Hit
G5 Gee Whiz (The Repairman No. 2)
Judge Jury Desert Fury (The Repairman No. 5)
Manhunter Series
No Good Deed (The Repairman No. 4)
Overflow (The Repairman No. 8)
Quiet Ops
Target Shy and Sexy (The Repairman No. 6)
The Bakken (The Repairman No. 3)
The Blue Pearl (The Repairman No. 10)
The K Factor (The Repairman No. 9)
The Repairman (The Repairman No. 1)
Venom
Who's on Top (The Repairman No. 7)

Contemporary:
Blood Lines
Unchained
Windfall

Non-Fiction:

Against the Grain

California Cocina
Cooking Wild & Wonderful
Cornucopia: Building A Greenhouse
Killing Cancer
The Write Stuff
Write Compelling Fiction (with Craig Martell)

Anthologies:

Paul Bishop Presents: Tales of Murder & Mayhem
The American West
The Trading Post
The Traditional West
The Manhunter Series
Western Fiction 10 Pack
Wolfpack Publishing Western Boxed Set
The Clint Ryan Series

Short Stories & Short Story Collections:

Holy Hell
Second is the First Loser
Short Story Collection & More
Slopes of the Sierra
Small Crimes
To Ride a Tall Horse
Western Short Story Showcase

I hope you gleaned even one iota of help from this short how-to, and go on to gain great success. As I said, you can't help others until you help yourself. God bless you and yours….

Join me:

http://www.ljmartin.com
http://www.facebook.com/ljmartinauthor

L. J. Martin

L. J. Martin

www.ingramcontent.com/pod-product-compliance
Lightning Source LLC
Chambersburg PA
CBHW021129070726
47591CB00014B/1901